By Pastor Lee Armstrong

cds@dsheriff.org
www.pastorleearmstrong.com   www.angelsatwar.com

FORWARD

In an hour when gender confusion is celebrated, a clear word on manhood is refreshing. Our culture seems bent on feminizing so much of our lives and institutions. To be masculine is to have qualities such as strength, boldness, courage, and bravery. Pastor Lee addresses these issues and more, with no apology or compromise. God is calling men to be men today in a time of moral decay. It is time for real men to step up to the plate, put on our "big boy pants" and make a stand for God.

Duane Sheriff, Senior Pastor

Victory Life Church
Durant, OK

DEDICATION

I dedicate this book to all the Real Men who choose to make a difference in our world. To all those men who are faithful to their wives, families, jobs, churches and country. To the Real Men who fight for the weak and discouraged, and give aid to those who are in need. To the Real Men who influence and mentor others out of a willing heart. To the pastors, teachers and ministers who refuse to give a watered down, re-heated, canned message. Who pray fervently for a relevant word from God.

To you, I dedicate this book, and I would like to say **"Well done, thou good and faithful servant"**!

In Christ,

Pastor Lee Armstrong

What Is A Real Man?

1) Original Design

2) How to Raise Real Men

3) Men are to be Respected

4) Defining a Real Man

5) He is Not Effeminate

6) He is a Lover

7) He is a Warrior

8) He is the Head

9) He Rules His House Well

10) He Blesses and Praises

11) He is the Provider

12) Real Men Make a Difference

Chapter 1

Original Design

Men and Women are different! No matter what you've been told or how many people try to change this, Men and Women are Different!!! You will never hear a man (a real man) ask, "Does this make my butt look big?" Men and women are different. You will never hear a man, a real man, ask, "Will you marry someone else, if I die before you?" Men and Women are different. You will never see men, real men, go to the bathroom in groups! Have you ever seen a girl jump on another girl's back just to show affection, or put their friend in a headlock? Men do that kind of stuff all the time. Why? Men and women are different. Men do not leave certain books out hoping you will read it! Men and Women are different, and we are different for a very simple reason; we were designed that way, by our creator. Have you ever noticed that even in lesbian and homosexual relationships one of the partners will take on the dominant male role and one will take on the submissive female role? This is because we know intuitively that someone has to lead! Perhaps "This is not about being better or superior, just responsible"! In our liberal society today there is great confusion about being a man, and what a real man looks like or is supposed to act like. We don't know if it's Arnold Schwarzenegger or Pee Wee Herman that we're supposed to be like.

Let's look briefly at some of the reasons we're confused:

#1) Global Information: We are inundated with stories from around the world about men who have five wives. That's just crazy; and in cultures where they marry at twelve & thirteen years of age, has caused many people to question our Judeo Christian Values.

#2) What's Become Socially Accepted: Everybody's doing it, so it can't be wrong! The whole Tolerance message has caused an everything goes, no holds barred, sociably acceptable mindset.

#3) Role Changes Are More Common: It was easy years ago to define a male and female because of their roles. Quite honestly, the man was the primary bread winner and the woman stayed home and invested her time in the children. Today, however many men stay home and watch the kids and the women work. This role reversal can cause confusion in the hearts of young people trying to find their way in life.

#4) Our Personal Experiences: If you were raised in one of those homes where the roles were reversed, you could be confused about being a real man. If your father was gone for any reason for great lengths of time, leaving you to spend all your time with mom and your sisters, you might struggle with your manhood as a result.

#5) Passive Preaching And Preachers: This is one I will take heat over but so be it! When we teach boys that God told us to turn the other cheek as a "good Christian" we imply, if not flat out proclaim, that they should not stand up for themselves or ever defend themselves under any circumstance, we emasculate them!! Boys are born warriors, aggressive, lionhearted, and willing to stand for what's right, or defend the weak or needy or even defend the faith. When we teach them to turn the other cheek without any balance, we absolutely pull the teeth out of that lion! I tell you unashamedly if you slap me, you better duck or run. I refuse to be a coward for Christ, or a sissy for Satan. I am a man, all man, very man, really man.

I'm here to tell you this world is confused, but God isn't! If we are going to push our way through the confusion and double standard that we are constantly being bombarded with through Hollywood and today's liberal media, we must look at the original design and, original intent of the Creator. If you don't understand the purpose for something you can mis-use the creation! For instance, have you ever used a cereal spoon for an ice cream scooper? It can be very frustrating; not because the creation is wrong but because it's not being used for its intended purpose! In the creation of anything, "Purpose Precedes Design". This means that what we create is created to meet a specific need. Bulldozers and Race cars have very little in common except that their purpose preceded their design; they were created entirely different because their purpose is completely different. We don't have bulldozer races for a reason, (they're very slow) they weren't designed to go fast, and their purpose (to push things down, to clear paths through the forests, etc.) preceded their design. A race car however was designed specifically to go fast, because purpose precedes design. This is such a vital truth that we must get a hold of before moving on. You and I were designed by our creator with a purpose in mind, and that purpose came before we were designed! On its most basic level, God purposed that you and I were to be a male or a female, and that purpose must be fulfilled for us to be truly happy in this life. We frustrate one another when we try to make our spouses or counterparts think and act like us. I know some of you struggle with feelings about someone of the same sex and I promise, I will deal with that at a later time in the book. The main point here is that men and women are different and that difference is by design, and God's purpose for you precedes your design. On a deeper level, you and I were designed to fulfill a higher calling that God purposed in you and I before we were even born, Read *Jer. 1:5.*

So let's take a look at God's original intent.

Gen. 1:26, "And God said, Let us make man (meaning **mankind**) in our image, after our likeness: and let them have dominion over the fish of the sea, and over the fowl of the air, and over the cattle, and over all the earth, and over every

7

creeping thing that creepeth upon the earth". Then in *verse 27*) "So God created man in his image, in the image of God created he him, male and female created he them". I must clarify a profound truth. When God created Adam, he placed in Adam all the attributes of the human species (male and female) or what we call mankind. Notice this again affirmed in *Gen. 5:2,* "Male and female created he <u>them</u>: and blessed them, <u>and called their name Adam,</u> in the day when they were created". We know this to be true again because God had to take Eve out of Adam via a rib and build her into the beauty we now call a woman! So whatever the Woman is, God took her out of the man and she became all that a woman is supposed to be, and Adam became all that a man is supposed to be, and they became <u>one</u> again through marriage. I do not have a feminine side! God took her out of Adam and built her into a woman that I call Ginger (my wife). My feminine side's name is Ginger and we've been happily married for almost three decades. If you try to teach me to crochet, I will stick that crochet needle in your thigh and show you a more excellent way. I am all man, really man, very man, and the liberal minded will just have to deal with it! This does not mean I drag my wife around the house by her hair. Quite the opposite, a real man honors his wife, and values her like he would the Hope Diamond "*1ˢᵗ Peter 3:7*". In *verse 28* of Genesis, chapter 1, the Bible says "And God blessed them, and the God said unto them, Be fruitful, and multiply, and replenish the earth, and subdue it: and have dominion over the fish of the sea, and over the fowl of the air, and over every living thing that moveth upon the earth". There it is! You and I are perfectly designed to have Dominion, to be Fruitful, and to Subdue the Earth. Why does it make you mad when the earth doesn't produce for you? Why does it frustrate you when you can't get rid of that ant problem? Because you were made to have dominion over such things and deep down inside you know it. Where we have dominion may differ, but men and women were created by God with this purpose in mind: to subdue, have dominion and be fruitful. We were also from the beginning designed to be different!

Seven Powerful Insights

1) God speaks the Vision before the man was created
   Gen. 1:26
2) God gives mankind himself *Gen. 2:7*
3) God shares the Original Vision with the man
   Gen. 1:28
4) God gives the man a job!
   Gen.2:15

   Why did he give him a Job? Because He's about to give him a wife!

5) God shows the man his need for life and love
   Gen. 2:16-18
6) God then meets that need
   Gen. 2:21, 22
7) God brings the woman back to the man and they became one again
   Gen. 2:22

Five Major Differences Between Men And Women

1) We walk different: Men walk with bravado, Men Lead (men truly dislike following)!

2) We talk differently: Men talk mostly facts. Women talk about feelings. Men are not always insensitive; they're just not going to cry about it. Crying doesn't help! Men communicate to gain respect. Women communicate to build relationships and, to be liked!

3) We act different: Men are naturally more aggressive. They push, shove, wrestle, and hit for FUN!!

4) We think differently: Men are firm, decisive, and logical.

Women are naturally more forgiving and able to flow with things.

5) We are physically different: No explanation needed.

Chapter 2

How to Raise a Real Man

Real Men do not become real men by osmosis, or by some magical, mystical transformation. They become real men by the involvement of other real men. Real men make a difference in their home, in their community, in their world. This I believe is why there's such a viscous attack on being a real man today. Have you noticed how men are portrayed in today's TV sitcoms and commercials? It's flat out embarrassing. Men are portrayed as absolute morons in these modern day depictions, barely able to tie their own shoes without a woman's help. Children openly make fun of their dad, calling him stupid and incompetent, while mom supports and even encourages this behavior. Long gone are the days when children called their dad their hero or mom looked at her husband as her knight in shining armor. While many people think these situational comedies are funny, I'm not laughing because I know that before evil can overcome a nation, the warriors and those that would fight for that nation must be removed. We will look at this in greater depth in the chapter on "Men are Warriors". I can't wait!

Five Things it Takes to Raise a Real Man

#1) A Mission
#2) A Mentor
#3) A Moment
#4) A Message
#5) A Multitude

#1) A Mission: This mission is to clearly define, "What is a real man?" No one builds a house without a blueprint, and no one wires that house without a schematic. That's because we know how important it is to clearly define from the start what we are going to build. The problem is, when I asked, not one person I spoke with could give me a decent definition of a man. Let me ask you. Can you to define what makes a man, a real man? At first the definitions were very superficial. I received answers like, "He's strong and He's courageous," but women fit these descriptions as well. You try staying home with four children, two of them under three years old. See for yourself (that takes courage)! Then there were action definitions, "He's a hunter, he goes fishing and camping. Again, many women fit these descriptions as well, and what's worse is that there are lots of real men who don't hunt or fish! So, I went on an intense Biblical search for an answer. Most of the remainder of this book will be dedicated to sharing those truths. For now let's at least conclude the need for those clearly defined Biblical definitions to raise real men. In *Hab. 2:2,* the Bible tells us why we need to write the vision down, and why we must make it plain. So our boys can see it, and then run with it! Our boys need to see God's vision for them. "For where there is no vision, the people perish", *Prov. 29:18.* The Bible also tells us to "train up a child in the way he should go, and when he is old, he will not depart from it." (*Prov. 22:6).* I hate pointing out the obvious, but the way that they should go is, "boys become Men and girls become Women!"

#2) A Mentor: Men beget men just like sheep beget sheep, and cows beget cows. Real men have had the influence of other real men in their lives. Paul said in *1ˢᵗ Cor.11:1* "Be ye followers of me, even as I am of Christ" and again in *2ⁿᵈ Thess.3:6-15* (especially verses 7, 9).Verse 7: "For ye yourselves know how ye ought to follow us". *Verse 9)* "not because we have not power, but to make ourselves an example unto you to follow us". Please take the time to read in *Gen. 18: 18, 19,* how God said he'd make a great nation out of Abraham, because he knew

Abraham would raise them up to keep the way of the Lord! A real man is a godly man; you and I will never be the man God intended us to be until we let God be a man in and through us. It takes Fathers, Grandfathers, Coaches, teachers, and many other male role models who will invest their time and influence into our boys to help form a real man mindset. Think about this for a moment, who had real influence in your life? I can assure you it wasn't politician, athlete, or an entertainer; it was individuals who took the time to get involved with you. Those people who taught you to fish, hunt, or play an instrument. Those precious individuals who spent countless hours teaching you to read, and write or understand what makes a thing work. These people are called mentors, and they are absolutely necessary for the framing and shaping of our minds and actions.

#3) It Takes Moments: It takes moments, defining moments, which we must be looking for diligently. Moments when our boys need affirmation that they have what it takes. Moments when they are told that they are more than enough, that they are men in the making. What's fascinating to me is that Jesus had these defining moments in his life! Let me remind you of just a few. How about when he was just twelve years old and he was left at the temple while his parents travelled three days before even missing him! Then there was his baptism by John. He comes up out of the water and the Spirit descends like a dove, then there's a voice from heaven saying "This is My Beloved Son, in whom I'm well pleased!" Talk about a defining moment; now think about that whole scenario for just one second. Jesus the Son of God was affirmed by his heavenly father (where others heard it)! If Jesus in his humanity needed affirmation, it's a sure thing our sons need it as well.

In many cultures these defining moments are built right into the fabric of their culture. Men spend their time teaching their sons the skills and knowledge they need to pass from being a boy into being a man. In one tribe, you leave the tribe and on your own you kill a lion. Then you will confirm this by the lion tooth necklace around your neck. Upon your return, you are then given the status of being a Man. In yet another culture, boys go through the painful right of passage of sticking their arm into an ant-infested hollow log, where they will be stung repeatedly by hundreds of angry ants. This is bad enough in and of itself, but even worse, if they are to pass this test they must endure this excruciating ordeal without any demonstration of pain!

These defining moments, while cruel to us, are moments these young men look forward to. Why? It's their public promotion to manhood!

What is Americas defining moment into manhood? Being able to buy beer! I want to propose that we begin to plan for and look for defining moments, moments where we can affirm them in the presence of others. Times when we plan to take them camping overnight, and we let them start the fire! John Eldrige and others have written wonderful books on this subject and given great examples of defining moments, let me share some examples that I've seen personally.

- Your child getting a good grade in a tough subject
- Overcoming a known fear of something
- Accomplishing a new responsibility
- The first time they spend their money on someone else
- When there is physical change: puberty!
- When they've sacrificed for the good of someone else

#4) A Message: Real Men have a code of ethics, which becomes a standard to live by; a message! That message comes from the word of God. Like the code of ethics mentioned in 1st *Cor. 13:4-8.* The "Love" chapter that reveals how to know when you're in love, what love looks like and how love expresses itself. Then there's the message of *1ˢᵗ Tim. 5:2- 3,* how to treat women. This moral message alone if lived out by young men would change the very fabric of our country. Our boys are like medieval knights in training and to become those knights they must have a code of ethics and standards that keep them on course.

#5) A Multitude: *Prov. 24:6,* "In the multitude of counselors there is safety." The more real men who can speak into your sons life, the better. When our culture honored the role of a man, and of a father, we did not have this much confusion simply because it was affirmed in the boys continually. In *Prov. 15:22,* the Bible once again confirms the power of multiple counselors helping establish spiritual truths. "Without counsel purposes are disappointed; but in the multitude of counselors they are established." This is why we need to find ways to get our sons around other real men. If you're a single mom get your son into church camp outings. Or ask some of the men in the church if they would be willing to spend time with your son. Most real men see this as a great honor and would love the opportunity to invest in the future of a young man.

Chapter 3

Men are to be respected

In today's effeminate world a real man is a modern day marvel! *Eph. 5:33* says "Nevertheless let every one of you in particular so love his wife even as himself; and <u>the wife see that she reverence (reverence; Def. **respect**) her husband.</u>" There are four definitions for the word reverence and those definitions reveal some wonderful truths.

#1) **To be in awe** (told you he's a modern marvel!)
#2) **To make to feel adequate**
#3) **To be honored or held in high respect**
#4) **To refrain from intruding upon**

#1) Real Men are a modern day marvel, something to be in awe of. When I see the difference between men and women lived out before me every day, I am in awe at this creation called Man. He innately see's life through his unique male perception of life; he can't help it. When I watch a young woman with her male counterpart having a meal together, and I see that sense of awe she has at this strange being across the table from her (called a man), I realize God is at work! Men need spouses that articulate often to their husbands that they're amazed at what he can do and sons who are encouraged to see their father as awesome, invincible, their hero.

#2) Behind every good man is a great women (someone who tells her husband he has what it takes, he's more than enough, he's the answer to the problem). When women do this they show respect, which makes them feel adequate and it becomes a prophetic word that comes to pass. It always amazes me how some women call their husbands names and then complain that he becomes what they have confessed him to be! A good woman knows that encouraging her husband and, boasting on his ability to get things done, absolutely empowers him to get things done.

#3) To be honored or held in high respect. When we honor someone it affects how we talk to them, what we say to them, and how we act around them. If someone you genuinely honor came to your house, wouldn't you want others to honor them as well? Wouldn't you want others to see them as valuable as you do? What if a child or acquaintance dishonored them? Wouldn't you be hurt? This is exactly how we should feel about our fathers and husbands, when someone (including us) dishonors them. When we truly understand the value of a man, then we honor them and treat them with respect!

#4) To refrain from intruding upon or interfering: This is a tough one for a lot of reasons, the least of which is that I will not be able to qualify and balance out every thought. So please give me some liberty here and I will try to share on this without sounding like I'm against women. One of the ways we show disrespect is by the simple act of interrupting people. In essence, interrupting someone when they are talking is like saying "please stop talking so I can tell you how smart I am, and show you how dumb you are"! Now we wouldn't come right out and say that but that's what we're saying. Wives who interrupt their husbands to correct the details of a story he is telling, are disrespecting him. I am like most men. I never intentionally lie to someone, but in the telling of a story I really don't care if it was Monday or Tuesday. I'm not as interested in 2:00 or 2:15pm as much as I am about the main point of the story! I really cannot remember all the details of my children's births. I do know they were born and their names (most of the time). Men tell stories differently than women, and that's Ok. When a wife asks her husband to discipline the kids and then interferes in the process of that correction, the wife is teaching the children to disrespect him, as well. I am not, however, talking about if he's abusing them, or doing something completely outrageous. Such things need to be challenged, but even then it can be done with respect.

Submission is one way you show your husband you respect him. I know, I know, I can hear it now, "but he hasn't earned respect. When he starts doing the right things, acting with respect toward me, then I'll show him some respect." I know we've been taught that respect is earned, and in most cases I would totally agree, however when it comes to the home and the husband, that's not how God sees it, and we need to be grateful, both male and female. Why? Because if the man has to earn her respect then the woman has to earn his love, and neither of those concepts are Biblically correct. Let's look at this according to God's word.

Eph. 5:21, "Submitting yourselves one to another in the fear of the Lord". We are to submit husband and wife to each other and to the Lord.

Eph. 5: 22, "Wives submit yourselves unto your own husbands, <u>as unto the Lord.</u>" The greater act of submission is on the wife, and she is to submit as if it was the Lord! Now this is very important so answer these questions carefully.

*Do you always understand what the Lord is doing or asking you to do?   Yes   or   No

*Do you always agree?   Yes   or   No

If you're completely honest you and I both know the answer to both questions is a resounding NO! No, we don't always understand the Lord's commands, and, no, we don't always agree, but we do submit. Why? This is because we know God's love for us and it makes us willing to submit. This is why the husband is asked to submit to God by loving his wife like Christ loves the church. *Eph.5:25* and *Eph. 5:33 says*, "Nevertheless let everyone of one of you **husbands**, in particular so love his wife even as himself; and the wife see that she reverence (**respect**) her husband". Therefore, we are to love and respect one another because God said so, and not necessarily because they earned it. This is what we call unconditional love and this is how God loves you and me! *1st John 4:11* confirms this idea: "Beloved, if God so loved us, we ought also to love one another". I know that loving and submitting to someone that doesn't deserve it is very hard, but it is what God has called us to, and it's where the love of God is best revealed. *Rom. 5:8,* "But God commendeth his love toward us, in that, while we were yet sinners, Christ died for us". So we respect the man (and love the woman) because God said to. Period!

Chapter 4

Defining the Man

This has been one of the hardest, most intense and yet very satisfying studies I have ever done. The reason, as mentioned earlier, is because the main descriptions we use are often way too superficial and insufficient to separate male from female. To say men are strong or courageous may be true but it is an incomplete and way too generic definition to raise from a boy to a man with. Remember we are looking for clearly defined Biblical definitions, and not our personal ideas or opinions. This is going to be really hard for some of us to get through, because those definitions are going to challenge us where we fall short, and some of those definitions create negative images. Let me demonstrate with one Biblical definition of a man: the man is "the head". This creates for many women an image of dictatorship or something even worse. God's definition of the head is not what most of us have been taught. So be patient and let the word of God set the record straight.

Exceptions to the rules don't change the rules. In these definitions and descriptions there will always be some men who talk more than their wives. However that doesn't change the scientifically known facts that on average a woman speaks approximately 25,000 words a day and a man speaks approximately 12,500 a day! Remember, exceptions to rules do not change the rules. It's interesting to know that sociologists wired a playground with microphones to listen to the interaction between children. Do you know what they found? Girls talked twice as much as boys! Guess what else they found? Most of the conversations the girls made were about building relationships, while most of the boy's vocal expressions were making noises (the bang, bang of gun fire, the noises of fire trucks and police cars, etc...). I'll bet that really surprises you! Another group took various kinds of toys (dolls, trucks, plastic guns, pots and pans) to a remote tribe who had never seen such things. Without any coaching from anyone, the girls naturally drifted to the dolls, and the pans, while the boys naturally drifted to the trucks and play weapons. That probably surprises you as well. You might say, the girls are used to seeing their moms using pots and pans, and the boys are used to seeing their dads using weapons. That only solidifies the point that even in remote areas where politically correct thinking could not affect their choices, girls will be girls and boys will be boys. In every culture I know of, the men are the aggressors, the warriors. They quite naturally are the leaders and quite naturally the women look to them for that leadership. This is scriptural and exactly what God said would happen. Notice *Gen. 3:16,* "Unto the woman he said, I will greatly multiply thy sorrow and thy conception; in sorrow thou shalt bring forth children; <u>and thy desire shall be to thy husband ,</u> and he shall rule over thee". The woman's desire shall be towards her husband. This means her **longing** shall be for her husband. This is why women ask," were you thinking about me today"? They have a longing for the man that God placed in them. Normally, if he was thinking about her today, it was not the kind of thinking she would want! I heard a woman ask a man, "do you think about anything besides sex" and he said, "Sure I do. I can't think about what it was right at the moment". Let's get real; it is primarily men who are hooked on internet pornography and primarily women who are hooked on internet chat rooms. This is because of how we're designed, and the enemy of our souls is trying to use our God-given design against us and, without God, it works all too well. It is men who made Playboy popular and women who made romance novels a billion dollar a year business. It is men who made the movie Braveheart famous and women who made the movie You've Got Mail famous. That's not bias, it's just the facts! The fact that we are different does not make anyone male, or female, superior to the other. It just helps us understand. When we recognize those differences, appreciate those differences, and then apply those differences, everyone wins.

Chapter 5

He is Not Effeminate

Whatever a man is he is **Not Effeminate** or, better said he is not a woman. God took Eve out of Adam. She was made from Adam's rib. The word "made" in "God made the woman" is defined as **built**. This means God built her out of the rib that was in Adam. We still use that term today when we find an attractive woman and we say she's built. {God took her out of Adam. How much of her? All of her!} So the man is now missing his feminine side (pun intended). Men, real men, do not have a feminine side unless they're married. At that point their feminine side has been brought back to them and they have become one again! Now notice what God's word has to say about our needs being different. *Gen. 2:24,* "Therefore shall a man leave his father and his mother, and shall <u>cleave</u> unto his wife: and they shall be one flesh". The word cleave used by God is not by accident, it shows us God's understanding of the difference between men and women. The word cleave, is one word with two distinct meanings, exactly like Adam was one man with two distinct characteristics. The first part of the word means **"cling to, adhere to, be joined to"**. It's what men call sex. The second part of the word means **"to follow after, to catch by pursuit".** It's what women call romance! Now everyone knows this to be true and yet we make fun of it, we have arguments over it, and have done so for thousands of years. The problem is that we may know the differences but we don't understand them, because they're not our needs. Men don't have flower withdrawals. Men don't have a need to be pursued! Women want to believe that their men would swim the deepest ocean, climb the highest mountain, and slay the dragon to save them, (and deep down so do men). It's romantic. Women don't generally have a need for sex, men do! A man can be so tired he doesn't have the strength or energy to take off his boots, but turn out the lights and he has more energy than she knows what to do with! One last testament concerning the difference between men and women, and sex: men can have a broke leg, one eye covered by a patch, an arm in a sling and still go to work and want sex.

Adam was alone in the garden, but he wasn't lonely until Eve was removed. God had to tell him that it wasn't good for him to be alone, because he wasn't lonely! She was in him and so he was complete. Without her, his perception is one sided (pun intended) and that side is masculine. If this was a man's world exclusively there would be no malls, only Bass Pro Shops. There would be no romance novels, only Popular Mechanics and Sports Illustrated Magazines, and this would be life. Women give us a woman's look at life which is completely different than the male picture.

Men are half brain-dead! Well that's kind of true, but a little incomplete concerning the facts. Women are bi-lateral thinkers meaning they go from the left hemisphere to the right hemisphere very easily. Men however, are primarily left-hemisphere oriented. The left hemisphere is where Conquer, Succeed, Dominate, and the Facts are located. The right hemisphere is where the Intuition and Emotions are located. This is why, when you say to a man, "we need to talk," his response will be, "about what"? When you ask a man, "how was your day"? Fine would be a great answer to another man, but this will seldom do when answering your spouse. Women are primarily right hemisphere bent which is why they want to know how you're feeling! They want to build relationships, get to know you and others, the facts are way too impersonal for them. When you ask a woman about a situation they will almost always say "I feel like we need to…", If however you ask a man the same thing he will almost always say "I think we need to…". The woman feels, the man thinks, and both are incomplete without the other. I heard a story of a couple in counseling and the woman was very upset and was really letting her husband know just how upset she was. When she turned to her husband and said, "You better get with the program, Bud": to which he responded, "There's a program?". Now that's funny. I don't care who you are!

A woman can cry and not necessarily know why. I promise you, if a man is crying he can tell you why! Women can cry when they're happy. They often judge a great movie by the fact that it made them cry. If I want to cry, I look at the bills, I don't go to the movies! I'm not saying men never cry, or that it's wrong for a man to cry. I'm saying women cry much more frequently and for lots of reasons a man would never understand.

Psalm 37:4, "Delight thyself also in the Lord; and he shall give thee the desires of thine heart". The words to delight thyself also means **to be soft**, **pliable**, **or effeminate**. If we stay soft, pliable, "effeminate", God can give us what's in our heart. This is because to be effeminate means to be like a woman, pliable, soft and quick to change her mind. This makes submitting to her husband a much easier thing to do. Now be honest, the man is not so quick to change his mind or his direction is he? You might call that being stubborn, but I have a question. What is the difference between being stubborn and being tenacious? Spelling! This, and whether you agree with the decision or not. Just like every one of us, our strengths are also our weaknesses and the main reason why we need each other.

Chapter 6

He is a Lover

A real man is a lover. He loves his wife, he loves his children, and he loves God. Notice he loves his wife and not someone else's wife. This is so important. You are not a lover if you're unfaithful; you're an adulterer! Faithfulness is an act of love for our spouses, for our children, and even for the world. Notice in *Eph. 5:25*, God said "Husbands, love your wives, <u>even as</u> Christ loved the church, and gave himself for it". The question we must ask ourselves then is "How did Christ love the church"? The answer to that is far too complex and deep to cover in this book (or any book for that matter) it must be experienced! We will look at just ten things that we as real men can learn and apply to our marriages.

Ten Ways to Love Like Christ

#1) Unconditionally: Christ loves the church unconditionally and that's how we're to love not just our wives and children but everyone. Likewise love is not earned by doing something but because God told us we should when he said we're to love her like Christ loved the church. We know we are to love the world with God's kind of love, but I think that no one should see the unconditional love of God more than our immediate family. The problem is, many people talk to their family in a way they would never talk to their neighbor and that's just not right! So we are to love our wife and kids at all times, when they burn supper, leave their rooms a mess, and even when they don't like us very much. [This is impossible to accomplish without God because you can't give what you don't have, and if you haven't received God's love for yourself, you can't give it to anyone else.] You might be a good man but without God you'll never be a godly man! God's unconditional love for the church was

24

based on who he was, not what they had done. So it is with your unconditional love. It will come from who you are, from your character and nature that you willingly give to others.

#2) Sacrificially: Jesus gave himself for His church, this is how God demonstrated His love. He was willing to give gifts to us (*Eph. 4:8, 11*) and he was willing to even die for us. Many men say they're willing to die for their wife and kids but they won't go to the mall with them, or even to the movies with them. I say unashamedly that every time I go to the mall, I die to myself. Every time I go shopping with my wife, I die to myself, and every time my wife goes to Bass Pro with me, (guess what?) She dies to herself as well.

One year at Christmas time, I wanted to do something special for my wife. Money was tight but my love was strong. I found out she wanted an expensive coat. We just didn't have it, but I did have a really nice guitar that I had owned for about ten years. Now only a true musician will understand the significance of this guitar in my life. Let's just say that this guitar was far more valuable than its monetary value (to me). I sold that guitar and took the money and bought her that nice coat. I have never regretted that decision. When you sacrifice for the benefit of someone else, you express and demonstrate God's love. If you have ever lived sacrificially for someone else, you know how rewarding showing that kind of love can be. When you take off work to go to your children's ballgame, or instead of going hunting for the weekend you stay and help with a sick child, you show sacrificial love. Love that has eternal ramifications!

When a man shows up in his home, his work place, his world as a man, he offers himself as a man. Our women, as great as they are, cannot teach our boy's to be men. Only another man can do that. Our boys need to see masculinity lived out, displayed and demonstrated. It cannot be learned from books alone. Like God, who offers Himself to us as God, we offer ourselves to those around us as men. Our sons need to test their strength against other men. This is why, if it's at all possible, you need to wrestle with your boys. They love this! It's an incredible day for a young man when he beats his dad at something, and it should be a great day for that dad as well.

#3) He Speaks the Word Over Her: A real man speaks the Word over his wife. He calls her what God calls her in his word. He calls her a "good thing" (*Prov. 18:22)*, he calls her "blessed" (*Prov. 31:28)*, He tells her she's the apple of His eye (*Zach. 2:8)*, He calls her His beloved (*Rom.* 9:25). He calls her all these things and more. He does not call her his (Old Lady), or his children (The Rug Rats). He calls those things that are not as though they are (*Rom. 4:17)*. It always amazes me what people call their spouses and then wonder why those spouses never reach their full potential and have a low self-esteem. The power of life and death are in our tongue and, like God, we must speak the word over our bride.

#4) He Presents Her to Himself: Presents her is defined as: **to stand beside, and before, to substantiate**. We prove and support the woman's role by being men, and we do this partially by standing beside them. How many times have our wives asked us to walk beside them? This is by divine design and if we're not walking beside them, we need to stand before them so we can lead and protect!

#5) He Loves Her Like He Loves Himself: A real man is not selfish in his dealings with his wife and children. This is something that I have never fully understood. How a man can spend $35,000.00 for a boat and then get mad at his wife for a $30.00 pair of shoes. God loves us as much as He loves His Son. (read *John 17:23)*. So He loves us like He loves Himself and He is our example. Our love for ourselves must never rise above the love we have for others! One of the problems we have fulfilling these roles is we don't have the same needs. Men do not have flower withdrawals, or pains. If we did, we would buy flowers more often. Do you know why men ask if you want to eat? They are hungry! Their stomach growled. The Truth is if they never got hungry you wouldn't eat. Women can see someone else get flowers or a card and they have flower withdrawals. They start feeling and thinking it's been 6 months since I got flowers and they feel real emotional pain. If men had that same pain, they would ask, "Do you want some flowers?" Now a man can't tell you the last time he bought flowers. He can't tell you the last time he bought you a gift. He can tell you the last time he had sex! Men and women are different.

#6) He Nourishes and Cherishes Her: The words nourish and cherish mean, **he helps her become all she can be to her fullest potential, and promotes her development**. A real man wants his wife to fulfill her destiny in God as much as he wants to fulfill his destiny in God. It means that it makes him happy when he thinks about her. In *Proverbs 31* ,the description of a virtuous woman is really intimidating to most women, and rightfully so. She is better than Wonder Woman. (Please read *Prov. 31:28.)* It reveals that the missing link for most of us concerning the virtuous woman is her husband. It says that he praises her and blesses her, and because he does so, her children grow up to bless her as well. I feel bad for a lot of men who work late not just for the money, but because they don't enjoy going home. It's easier to stay late at work than it is to deal with the problems in their relationships at home. I love going home, I love my family's excitement upon my arrival. It's fulfilling to know my wife is glad to see me, and my son is ready to wrestle! That doesn't happen by accident. I have worked through some very difficult situations to get where we are now. Things like the death of my daughter, my son's eighteen year battle with Hyperplastic Left Heart Syndrome which means the whole left part of his heart never developed, and that's the small stuff! The point is, we have worked through all these things by God's nourishing and cherishing love that He has for us, and our giving that back to each other.

#7) He Gives Her Gifts: I don't know a woman yet that doesn't love getting gifts. In *Eph.4:8,* the scriptures tell us that God gave the church gifts; Pastors, Teachers, Evangelists, Apostles, and Prophets. Did you know that? Do you understand that your Pastor is a gift from God to you and your church? I'm so grateful to God for my Pastor and for these ministry gifts. Even more so that God gave them to me! This is a wonderful truth about God and the church, and you and your spouse. Every woman has a thing that she loves to receive as a gift. For some women it's flowers, for others its porcelain dolls, or angel figurines. I even know a woman who just loves power tools! Whatever it is, be sure to give her gifts often and not just when it's her birthday, anniversary, or when you've messed up. It is one of the things that attracted her to you in the first place. If we would treat each other like we did when we were dating, our marriages would sure benefit in a very positive way!

#8) He's Faithful to Her: God is so faithful to us, even when we're not so faithful to him. God never thinks, "I wish I never would have saved that one". His heart is always grateful for our relationship with him. In *1ˢᵗ Tim. 3:12,* the Bible says to the men "Let the deacons be the husband of one wife". Now if you've missed the mark in this area there is still hope and there is still the power of God to restore and to heal, but it's much easier to stay faithful than it is to overcome broken trust. A real man is not just faithful in his marriage by not having a physical affair, but he's faithful to her with his eyes and his mind. He doesn't flirt with his female co-workers to stroke his ego. He doesn't look at pornography or stare at the cute new girl in the office letting his thoughts run amuck. He brings those thoughts into captivity by the word of God. He looks for excitement in his wife and if it's not there, he takes responsibility to re-kindle that excitement. He dates his wife, and tells her how beautiful she is, and how he longs for her!

#9) He Delights in Knowing Her: *1ˢᵗ Peter 3:7,* "Likewise, ye husbands, dwell with them (your wives) according to knowledge, giving honor unto the wife, as unto the weaker vessel, and as being heirs together of the grace of life; that your prayers be not hindered". God says that eternal life is not so much a place as it is us knowing God, and His Son Jesus Christ *(John 17:3)* whom he sent. We are creatures of relationship and God wants us to live with our wives and get to know them. One of the ways that God shows his love for you is by knowing you better than you know yourself. My wife is continually throwing me a curve: I think I know her and then she does something that absolutely stuns me. This is why marriage is a great adventure: you never know what's around the next corner! Our wives delight in us wanting to know them, I mean really know them. This brings them great security in the relationship, just as we have with God the more we know him.

#10) He Takes Responsibility: Christ did what Adam didn't do in the garden, he takes responsibility. Adam did not take responsibility for his home or his marriage. He actually did just the opposite; he tried to blame his wife for the whole thing. There's a little Adam in all of us isn't there? I love the whole redemptive story of Christ and the Cross *but one of the most amazing aspects of the cross is Jesus taking responsibility for my mistakes*. Real men do not let their wives talk them into things they know they can't afford and then get angry and blame them for the problem! If you're going to be a real man, a godly man, then say "no" to things you don't agree with, and take responsibility for the outcome (good or bad). That is what God did. He said no to Adam and then took responsibility to fix Adam's mistake. How powerful is that? Being the head of your house does not make you better than, just responsible for!

Chapter 7

He's a Warrior

Real men want to fight! They are warriors who are looking for a dragon to slay, an evil wizard to oppose, and a fair maiden to save. Men love Braveheart, Gladiator, and John Wayne! They love the underdog winning against all odds and they see themselves as the hero in every story, and this starts at a very early age. You can try to keep all weapons away from your boys. You can forbid all family members from buying any aggressive toys, and those boys will make a spear out of a broom handle and slay an imaginary dragon! They will chew a cracker into the shape of a gun. Men are innately inclined to fight and, as discussed previously men are naturally more aggressive, more competitive, and more confrontational than women. Men are going to fight!

Three Ways Men Will Fight

1) They will fight against you
2) They will fight with you
3) They will fight for you

#1) They Will Fight Against You: In *James 4:6,* the Bible tells us that "God resisteth the proud, but giveth grace unto the humble." This means God fights against the proud. It literally means **he opposes you**. That's an eye opener, the thought that God might be opposing you, fighting against you because you're in pride. If God will fight against you under certain situations, it shouldn't be a surprise that men will fight against you under certain situations as well. If a man is fighting the devil for his family and his wife opposes him in whatever decision he makes, then the battle is no longer between him and Satan. The battle is now shifted to between him and his wife, and the only one winning will be the devil! It has always intrigued me how women want their husbands to lead as long as the husbands lead like the wives want them to! The problem is, this will cause a fight but it will be between the wife and him and not the Devil and him!

#2) They Will Fight With You: In *1ˢᵗ Cor. 3:9,* the Bible teaches that we are "labourers together with God". God is working with us; it is God working in and through us that allows us to be successful in our Christian efforts. In *Phill.2:13*, the Bible shows this very clearly "For it is God which worketh in you both to will and to do of his good pleasure". Like God, the man will work with you if you'll let him, he desires to see his strengths used in union with her strengths to build a house that they mutually benefit from. He strives to use his masculine strength matched with her feminine touch. He loves the power tools and tearing out walls but seldom enjoys or cares about the type of curtains she wants. He wants to know how he can help and loves it when his spouse works with him.

#3) They Will Fight for You: In *1ˢᵗ Sam. 17:47*, the scriptures teach that "the battle is the Lords". This is one of the greatest truths in scripture concerning you, me and spiritual warfare. The truth is, we have no human weapons with which to fight the devil. All our weapons are from God and of God. Notice *2ⁿᵈ Cor. 10:4-5* "For the weapons of our warfare are not carnal, but mighty through God to the pulling down of strong holds" *(verse 5)* "Casting down imaginations, and every high thing that exalteth itself against the knowledge of God, and bringing into captivity every thought to the obedience of Christ". So we have a battle to fight and a dragon to slay, and a fair maiden to win, but the only way to truly win is to let God fight the battle for us. The best we can do is to obey his word, and stay out the way!

Adam's failure was Christ's victory. In the garden when Adam and Eve were tempted of the devil, there was a time between when Eve had eaten the forbidden fruit and Adam had not. We don't know just how long that time was, but that there was time. In *Gen. 3:6,* here's what it says "…She took of the fruit thereof, and did eat, and gave also to her husband with her, and he did eat." Somewhere between when she ate and when he ate he should have said NO! He should have fought for her and sanctified her with his righteous choice according to *1st Cor.7:14,* "For the unbelieving husband is sanctified by the (believing) wife, and the unbelieving wife is sanctified by (believing) husband: else were your children unclean; but now are they holy" *parenthesis added.* In those few moments Adam was still obedient to God and Eve was not. He could have stood up for her, defended her, and even sanctified her with his choice of staying obedient to Gods Word. In essence he could have slayed the dragon, but he didn't. He listened to his wife and not God! This same scenario is played out in the world over and over again between thousands of couples and many other relationships, as well. Every time someone listens to man instead of God! When a pastor listens to his congregation instead of God, this Garden of Eden mistake is repeated. Men can save their families from the dragon by truly leading them in obedience to God's Word and plan but this is not easy or popular. Obeying God often puts us at odds with the multitudes and creates an attitude in many that we are the problem. That's why it takes a warrior's heart to see it through. It is an indictment against us as men to know how many times we let our wives or children talk us into what we know in our heats is a wrong choice!

The good news is that Jesus Christ, the Captain of the Lord of Hosts, is our mighty warrior, and he will fight our battle for us, if we will just obey. Notice these scriptures and remember that God is no respecter of persons. What he did for others he will do for you. In *1st Sam. 17:47,* the story of David and Goliath, David is addressing this giant Philistine and he's telling this giant called Goliath that the Lord's going to deliver him into his hands and that he is going to be buzzard bait. Then he says this in *verse 47,* "And all this assembly shall know that the Lord saveth not with sword and spear: <u>For the battle is the Lord's,</u> and he will give you Philistines into our hands". It was not the rock that killed Goliath, **but the God of the rock**! Then there's the story in *2ⁿᵈ Chron. 20:15* where God gives this promise "And he said, Hearken ye, all Judah, and ye inhabitants of Jerusalem, and thou King Jehoshaphat, Thus saith the Lord unto you, Be not afraid nor dismayed by reason of this great multitude; <u>For the battle is not yours, but God's</u>". Wow! Doesn't that encourage you? Doesn't that make you want to sing a song, like the one David sang in *Ps.3:6,* "I will not be afraid of ten thousands of people, that have set themselves against me round about"? If we are under spiritual siege today, we can rest in God because he is willing to fight the battle for us! We are created in God's image and like God, this is what real men want to do, they want to fight for you! That's why if you say there's a problem, they want to know who, what and where, because then they can go take care of it. If you tell a real man about some problem, but can't tell him what you want him to do to fix it, you will thoroughly frustrate him.

Evil thrives when good men do nothing! The Devil certainly knows this and has capitalized on it repeatedly. There's an incredible story of what it takes for evil to take place in a kingdom, country, or home. You must first remove the warriors. Those who would oppose evil or cause you resistance. In *2ⁿᵈ Kings 24:11-19,* King Nebuchadnezzar overtook King Jehoiachin and began to remove all the items of value and then he removes the real problem involved in taking a country: the warriors. Notice *verse 14,* "And he carried away all Jerusalem, and all the princes, and all the mighty men of valour, even ten thousand captives, and all the craftsman and smiths : none remained, save the poorest sort of the land," and again in *verse 16,* "And all the men of might, even seven thousand, and craftsman and smiths a thousand, all that were strong and apt for war, even them the king of Babylon brought captive to Babylon" and then the king of Babylon made Zedekiah king in his place. Then there's this statement in *verse 19,* "<u>And he did that which was evil in the sight of the Lord, according to all that Jehoiakim had done</u>". That's how it works in every location, whether that location is a country, a government, a business, a school or a home! The enemy must eliminate anyone who would stand against them; I believe this is the real agenda behind this feministic push in our culture. If all the men (the warriors) are reduced to impotent mindless idiots that the Hollywood elite would like you to believe they are, who is there to stand in their way?

In verse 14, the term "*carried away*" means to **denude**, **to strip**, **to exile**, which is exactly what they did. They stripped them of their rank, power, authority, dignity, glory and grace. They were disgraced in every way possible. This is exactly what is being done today to the mighty men, the valiant men, those apt for war. They are being denuded on every front; they are being stripped of dignity, power, grace, authority and rank. The picture being painted of men in commercials and sitcoms today is atrocious. It would seem that any man in media today is a complete moron, incapable of even tying his shoes without a woman's help. You have to go back many years to find a show where the man was man and his wife and children respected him for being so. Does Little House on the Prairie or The Walton's ring a bell with anyone? In these shows, respect from the wife and children for the man were a common thread and often the main theme of a particular episode. Today the object of almost all sitcoms is to show how stupid men are, how women rule the roost, and how absolutely incapable men are to lead. We're being denuded!

Notice the type of men who were taken away before evil could prevail.

*All Jerusalem: A reference to those that made Jerusalem "Jerusalem", they were the DNA of Jerusalem.

- Princes: Strong's # 8269 Def. A head person, (of any rank or class), Chief Captain (that had rule), General, Governor, Keeper, Lord, or Ruler

- Mighty Men of Valor: Strong's # 1368 Def. Powerful: By implication Warrior, Champion, Giant Man, Mighty (man/one), Strong man, Valiant man
- Craftsman/Smiths: A Fabricator of any material, Carpenter, Craftsman, Engraver, Maker, Skillful, Worker, Workman
- Those that were Apt for War: To do or make war, battle, to fight or engage

When you take all the skilled labor, the craftsmen, the carpenters and the leaders at all social levels, you will leave only the poorest sort, which by definition means the poor and needy. That's exactly what happens to any location where the warriors, rulers and leaders are removed. Our whole social structure is in jeopardy today because there are not enough warriors; men to stop the evil that's being promoted by wicked godless people.

It is so vital that all the men (males) young and old respond to their God- given role as a warrior. When they do, everyone benefits including the men! We need real men today to take a stand for Christ publicly, to help their families work through the death of a loved one, to be courageous enough to fight for the spiritual well-being of their children, to start a new business, or go overseas as a missionary. All of these things and more are what we all know takes a real warrior attitude to accomplish, and while there's a part of all men that would take the easy way out, there is another part of you that yearns to pass the test. Real men do not promote fighting, but neither do they teach their children to run from a bully. If my son gets a suspension from school for defending himself, or better yet defending someone smaller who's being injured by a bully, we will celebrate his courage and go fishing! If your son is being picked on by someone at school don't teach him or tell him to turn the other cheek. Teach him to stand up and defend himself. The truth is, even if he loses the fight he'll gain his self-esteem, and self-respect, and the bully will find someone else to torment.

Most women are going to really struggle with this concept for several reasons but mostly because they believe this is not a Biblically correct concept. It's really hard for us to understand that Jesus could do anything like that, but he could and he did and it's in the Bible! In *John 2:15,* the scriptures tell a very seldom repeated story as it happened. Jesus went to the temple to worship and found people making financial profit by cheating and stealing from God's people. What you hear little about is that he made a whip and drove those people out of the temple and he wasn't nice about it. Now this action by Christ causes great stress for most pastors and religious leaders, let alone the common Christian believer. Add to that the cultural swing toward a tolerance message that even the church has adapted so that all we ever hear about Jesus is His love expressed by compassion. The problem is, love is expressed in many other emotions and actions. "For whom the Lord loveth he chasteneth, and scourgeth every son whom he receiveth" *(Heb. 12:6).* So love is expressed in the disciplining of child! Our children would say that's not very tolerant, but it is love. When someone stands up and fights for the underdog and wins, we consider that an act of love unless it's a Christian standing up for himself. What's really hard to explain is the fact that Jesus took the time to build the whip he used. That's pre-meditated aggression! Jesus was not tolerant. I'm not promoting violence or that Jesus was a spiritual Rambo. Just that being a man demands that we understand the Bible teaches Jesus was a man, a real man and not some tolerant pacifist.

Chapter 8

He's the Head

"For the husband is the head of the wife, even as Christ is the head of the church: and gave himself for it", *Eph.5:23,* this is God's word. I don't care if that makes people mad, or if it's not politically correct, I care that its Biblically correct. Being the head doesn't mean the man is better than or superior to, it just means he's responsible for! When God deals with a family, a group or even a nation he deals with the head. In the garden, when Adam and Eve had eaten the forbidden fruit, who did God deal with first? You guessed it; the head, "Adam". *Gen. 3:9* "And the Lord God called unto Adam, and said unto him, "Where art thou"?

The word "*head*" in the Old Testament means **the captain, the high priest, the principle ruler.** In the New Testament the word "head" means the part most readily taken hold of. This is a real man's innermost desire, to be the Captain of his ship, the High Priest of his home, the Principle Ruler. When the head is dysfunctional, the whole body feels the effects. The enemy understands this and I believe this is why there is such an attack against the man being the head. If he can't stop the man from being the head, he will attempt to distort this concept. Have you noticed the distorted view of men on today's TV shows? Name one show that's not 20 years old where the man is portrayed as something other than a complete mess up. Better yet, name one where the man is actually intelligent and morally grounded and his family respects him. This is not by accident as much as it's a well-executed plan to distort the man and his God-given role as the head. Without a real understanding of God's word, being the head can be seen as dictatorship or something worse! It's my desire to bring back the role of a man as a positive image in people's minds, and the families once again see their man as their hero and knight in shining armor.

Wives love it when the man is the High Priest of his home and he takes the children to church even when she doesn't go! Wives love it when their husbands lead. But if husbands won't lead, they will. Their need for security will ultimately bring them to the place of taking control, even though they don't really want to. They will not let their kids go to Hell because the husband won't be the High Priest. If necessary, they will be the spiritual leader, but it's not their desire! I love the balance that the Word of God brings to everything, including our homes and marriages. We are told that the man is the head ***Even As Christ*** is the head of the church: and he is the saviour of the body. So the question is "Are you leading like Christ?". This principle in God's word is called the Even As Principle. It's a comparison that helps us keep things in balance. We are to be the head of our family like Christ is the head of his family. If women understood what it means to be the head they wouldn't want it. Being the head means you're out front, leading the way, taking the enemy's attack first. Like the heads of the army, you're the one with bulls-eye on your forehead.

In practicality, being the head means you call the creditors when you're going to be late on a payment. Only cowards make the wife call! The real question is" How does Christ lead the church?" And how does He get the church to follow His leading? The answer to those questions will change your whole family structure and the way your family responds to your leadership. Jesus is the head because He submitted to His heavenly Father and did only what He saw His Father do. Jesus showed us His love and that love caused us to be willing to submit to His leadership and His leading. This is our example and should be our goal as the head of our household: to do only what our Heavenly Father does and be totally submitted to him.

The problem is, even in the body of Christ there are way too many involuntary body movements, movements that didn't come from the head! Here's where the rubber meets the road; where we flesh it out, and walk it out. I don't know a man who, if asked, wouldn't say he was willing to die for his wife and kids. The problem is, when we won't go to the mall or the movies, or their baseball games with them: it sends a very different message. I die to myself every time I go to the mall or the movies or when I stay home instead of going hunting or fishing. When I rearrange my schedule to make a ballgame, or spend the money I was going to buy a new bow with and buy my wife a new couch instead. I know this is hard to swallow but our excuses are nothing more than just that, *excuses*. Even though we have many and they're all very real and even seem right to us, they are excuses. I am busy making a living, I don't like the movies, I can't stand the mall, I, I, I. Therein is the real problem; how often the word "*I*" becomes the determining factor. Real men think in terms of responsibility for the whole, not just what's best for them. That's a part of what makes them real men! A very wise man once said people who are good at making excuses are seldom good at anything else. Be a real man. Be the head even as Christ is the head!

Chapter 9

He Rules

A real man rules! It starts in Genesis and runs all through the scriptures. Look at *Gen. 3:16,* "Unto the woman he said, I will greatly multiply thy sorrow and thy conception; in sorrow thou shalt bring forth children; and thy desire shall be to thy husband, <u>and he shall rule over thee</u>". I know what you're thinking," But that's Old Testament." That's true but some things came through the cross and were forever changed (the sacrificing of bulls and goats), and some things came through the cross and stayed the same (men ruling), and I'll prove it. Let's make sure that the rest of the scripture is still accurate and true today as it was when it was written. Then we'll know if it came through the cross and changed, or came through the cross and stayed the same. Let's answer some questions about this verse. Do women have sorrow bringing forth children? The answer's "yes!" Second question: "Is a woman's desire to her husband?" This means: is her longing for her husband? Before you answer, let me ask you something. Is it the man or a woman who asks, "Were you thinking about me today?" It's the woman because her desire is for her husband. So if those things are true, and they are, then so is the part about the husband ruling over her. In *1ˢᵗ Tim. 3:4-5*, we read concerning the office of a bishop, that he is "One that <u>ruleth</u> well his own house, having his children in subjection with all gravity;" *verse 5* "For if a man know not how to <u>rule</u> his own house, how shall he take care of the church of God". Notice again (verse 5) "For if <u>a man</u> know not how to <u>rule</u> his own house", that's New Testament! Men were designed by God to rule, the balance of that is in the rest of the scripture where a man ruling his house is defined as him taking care of his house. Notice the comparison between ruling his own house and taking care of the church. This is what it means to rule well: it means you're responsible to take care of those in your household. The truth is your wife and children are looking to you to take care of them, to make them feel safe and in need of nothing. It's in the home that you learn how to be a good minister. Raising a family is basic training for ministry. It's in the home we learn how to disagree agreeably; we learn to work together as a team, to use individuals in their strengths and to delegate their weaknesses. It's where we are to learn how to deal with authority, and how to submit to authority. The home is the perfect place to learn how to deal with criticism, murmuring and complaining, and disappointments.

Truths to Learn About Ruling

1) To rule is to stand before. In rank
Example; Like a General, or Captain in the army

- The man is out front
- The man leads into battle
- The man is the example to the family

2) His Children are in Subjection. They are lower in rank! It means they follow. They're not supposed to lead but with today's liberal mindset where children sue their parents and the goal is to make them happy, I'm going to sound archaic. We have evolved to a place where we now schedule our adult life and activities around our children's lives. I know of moms who get up and cook their children's breakfast only to be told "I don't want that," so the mom asks them what they want her to make, only to be rejected again! I have an idea. Let them not eat the first thing you make and don't make them anything else until lunch! I can almost guarantee you two things. First, they will eat what's for lunch. Second, they won't be so quick to turn down tomorrow's breakfast. If they want a $150.00 pair of shoes, we feel obligated to buy them. It would be unthinkable to make them work for them, as if we're some kind of horrible parent for wanting them to learn the real value of something! I have an idea that may cause resistance at first from the kids but what if God was smart enough to put parents in charge because they had already experienced being a child and knew what the children needed and not just what they wanted! Let's look at some of the problems that come with letting the children rule.

* **Empty Nest Syndrome:** This particular problem is based entirely upon grownups living their lives for their children. They build their entire life around making the children's lives enjoyable. In this scenario, parents choose their children over their marriage and each other. The truth is, the very best thing you can give your children is a great marriage where they learn by example how two people in love really treat each other.

* **The Blind Leading the Seeing:** It's bad enough that the blind lead the blind, but when we let our children make the decisions, we are in essence letting the blind lead those of us who can see. Not only is that absurd but it also puts the whole family in the direction of being totally dysfunctional.

* **Frustration for the Whole Family:** When the children are in charge, the whole family becomes increasingly frustrated and disorganized. This is because children know nothing of responsibility unless you teach them and, if you do that, you're ruling your own house well! If you do not want to eat at McDonald's, then don't ask the children where they want to eat. Just take them to your favorite place and teach them to eat what has been so graciously put in front of them.

* **Rebellion to God's Word:** It is God who said the man was to rule his own house well, and anything else is disobedience and rebellion to God's Word. If you want the blessing of God in

and on your home then you must line up with his divine design for the home.

3) Their Children are in Subjection With All Gravity: They follow out of respect given because of age, wisdom and character. Requiring your children to respect you is **not** a dictatorship. **It's good leadership**. Our children need to follow because we're older, because we have wisdom, and because we have character; not because we are a character! Being older does not automatically make us wiser and of good character, but it does give us an advantage in these areas. There are things we know from experience and different situations that give us the edge no matter how book- smart our children are. It is to their benefit to respect you for all these things, if for nothing more than that it's good seed to sow.

In *1ˢᵗ Tim. 5:17,* the scriptures encourage us to "Let the elders that <u>rule</u> well be counted worthy of double honour, especially they who labor in the word and doctrine". I love the fact that God knows the difference between those who rule and those who rule well. Here we're told to give them twice as much honor, because of the work in the word and in doctrine. When a pastor or leader rules well, he or she works hard to study and to show themselves approved unto God, and to be of sound doctrine. For them to do so will undoubtedly cause them to suffer persecution and rejection for the words sake. In *Hebrews 13:17,* once again we are instructed to "Obey them that have the <u>rule over you</u>, and submit yourselves; for they watch for your souls, as they that must give account, that they may do it with joy, and not with grief: for that is unprofitable for you". There are those that rule over us; fathers in the Lord, mentors, and spiritual leaders, and they watch for our souls. They do this knowing they must give an account meaning "God will hold them accountable for how they handle us." *Matt. 18:6,* comes to mind, "But whoso shall offend one of these little ones which believe in me, it were better for him that a millstone be hanged about his neck, and that he were drowned in the depth of the sea." Ouch! Now that's accountability! The reason you can obey and submit is the knowledge that they will give an account.

Another reason is so that they can lead us with joy and not with grief. It is not to our benefit if our leaders are mad or sorrowful or frustrated with leading us. Remember when Moses was angry at the children of Israel and asked God to kill him because of it (*Num. 11:15*)? That's a perfect example of this scripture coming to pass in the life of Moses. He was so frustrated at trying to lead these people who complained about everything all the time that leading was just not worth the effort. He despaired even of life itself, which is a really bad place to put your leader in, and then to expect anything good to come from it is crazy! Besides, all this obeying and submitting to those who have the rule over us is really good seed to sow.

Chapter 10

He Blesses and Praises

Real men have enough strength to boast and brag "*on others*"! This is a character attribute that separates real men from the multitude of men. In *Prov. 31:28,* speaking about the virtuous women, "Her children arise up, and call her blessed: <u>her husband also, and praiseth her</u>." Now I ask you. Is it natural for your children to call their mom blessed? Not in most homes. But this scripture tells us why these children rise up and bless their mom. Notice the rest of the verse: "her husband also, and praiseth her". What does that mean: "her husband also? It means her husband also calls her blessed! The father has taught the children by example. He calls her blessed so the children call her blessed. That's how it's supposed to be: the husband leads the family in a willingness to bless others. He not only calls her blessed; he praises her as well. "Praiseth her" is defined as: to be clear, to rave, to boast, to celebrate. Do you see that your praise cannot be vague or ambiguous? It is to be clear. If she has to guess or read between the lines, it's not praise. When you clearly boast on her, rave about her, and celebrate her, then you praise her. If you do this when you're around others it's even better. I have seen a lot of men make fun of their wives, ridicule their wives and even openly embarrass them and then chasten them for getting their feelings hurt. This is not what we're called to as real men; we are to be our family's greatest fans. It's up to us to be the one who celebrates their victories and boasts on their accomplishments. Our children act like they don't care for us hollering their name at a ballgame or cheering them on at a track event, but don't you believe it. They love it and they need it. Real men supply that!

The blessings of the family were passed down through the father! He laid hands on his children and spoke a blessing over them. In *Gen.27: 27-40,* Jacob cheats his brother, Esau, out of his blessing by deceiving their father into believing he was blessing Esau. It was far more than just some religious ceremony. It was obviously important and real to Jacob and Esau because once the deed was done Esau begs his father for a reserved blessing. Listen to his final plea to his father (*verse 38*), "And Esau said unto his father, Hast thou but one blessing, my father? Bless me, even me also, O my father. And Esau lifted up his voice, and wept". It's interesting to note that everything Isaac their father spoke over them came to pass just as he spoke it. In *Gen. 48:14-22*, Israel blesses his grandchildren by laying his hands on them and speaking a blessing over them. In *Gen. 49:1-28,* Jacob blesses his twelve children, and tells them what will happen to them.

The bottom line is, wonderful things happen when real men lay hands on their family and speak the word of God over them. In *Heb. 6:1-2* the Bible teaches us that the principle of the laying on of hands is a doctrine of Christ! That is going to surprise many Christians because many have been taught that it's a doctrine of Charismatics. Even more revealing is what *Mark 10:13-17* shows us. Many adults brought their children to Jesus that "he might touch them". The disciples rebuked them for bothering Jesus, and Jesus rebuked the disciples and told them to let the children come to him. Then in *verse 16,* he shows us what the parents were wanting from him "And he took them up in his arms, put his hands upon them, and blessed them". Real men follow Christ's example and lay hands on their children and bless them!

One more thing to further establish the power of laying hands on people and speaking a blessing over them comes from *1st Tim. 5:22*. The scriptures teach us to "lay hands on no man suddenly". The apostle Paul tells us to be patient about laying hands on individuals for ministry too quickly because spiritual things are imparted and the gifts and talents of God are without repentance. If nothing happens when spiritual leaders place their hands on people, then why the warning? Real men take these scriptures seriously and understand it's up to them to speak the blessings and praises over their family.

Chapter 11

He is the Provider

Real men know and understand that they are the provider, and that means more than providing just money! In *1ˢᵗ Tim. 5:8,* here's what the scriptures have to say about men providing, "But if any provide not for his own, specially for those of his own house, he hath denied the faith, and is worse than an infidel". Notice what it didn't say (that we've been told that it said). It didn't say he provides just money. Providing nothing but money for your family is called alimony and that's no laughing matter. Our sons need more than a credit card, or even an allowance, they need a godly example, and a man to wrestle with. Boys want to test their strength against another man. I have had dozens of boys at the house and it never fails that when I start wrestling with my son they want to join in. They love this time of wrestling and I make sure to provide it. It's been something that all those boys want to do every time they come over. Only another man can provide the masculinity that the boys need so badly. As good as Momma is, she can never be a true masculine role model. We provide our strength to our wives and children: our physical strength and our strengths as males, our factual thinking, our decisive way of looking at things, and our logical interpretations in any given situation. We intrinsically know we're supposed to provide and we feel the pressure of this constantly. I know big men, real men, the man's man type of individuals who were brought to tears after losing their job and not being able to find another one.

I know women don't feel this pressure of providing in the same way a man does. Evidence of this is demonstrated in the things they ask for and talk about. A woman will start talking to her husband just to talk to him, and start asking for things. She doesn't believe she's asking for things, but that's how the man hears it. The conversation goes something like this: (Her) I would sure like to go to Hawaii someday. (His interpretation) That's $5,000.00. (Her) We sure need a new car. (His interpretation) That's $18,000.00, (Her) and the house sure seems small with the two kids growing like weeds. (His interpretation) That's $150,000.00! The truth is, sometimes they are hinting, but most of the time they're just talking! They don't feel the pressure of providing for all those things, because they're just talking. However, real men do.

Another example of this is their requests often cancel each other out. For instance, she will say. "we need to spend more time together", and in the same breath share how the electric bill is three times the normal rate so we will have to put in some overtime to cover it. That message is interpreted through the ears of, "We need to provide that!" Remember real men are geared to slay the dragon, to fight the battle, and win the fair maiden.

Chapter 12

Real Men Make a Difference

Real men make a difference. What they do matters. They have impact and influence. They make a difference in their home, their church, their community and even in their country. The statistics concerning the difference a man makes in the home are overwhelming. The jails are filled with men and women whose lives are the by-product of having no father in the home. Missing fathers are one of the main reason for poverty and crime in our country. Ed Cole says it this way, "Absentee fathers are causing society to pay a high price for their low living". I agree. Their absence has a rippling affect on the fabric of all human activities. There are others who, in the absence of a real man, struggle in their masculinity, looking to be affirmed as a real man. Homosexuality, in simplicity, is a man's need for male influence in his life that has become completely twisted and contorted. This is just one of the problems in our society that we could change if we would just be what God called us to be (real men). I run into men everywhere who are still trying to get their fathers to affirm them, still trying to accomplish enough, be successful enough that their fathers would say, "I'm proud of you!" . It is so fundamentally life-changing to know you're the man, to know you have what it takes. I wrote this book in part to do just that. To tell you that you're the man and that if you will obey God you can be the catalyst for change. That change could affect your whole family and their destiny, which in turn affects your community, country, and ultimately your world. You can be a real man whose time on this earth counts for something valuable because there is a dragon to slay, a wizard to defeat, and a fair maiden to be won. You were born for such a time as this. Can you hear the voice of God calling you to something more than just existence? There's a big world out there in need of real men who know who they are and why they are here. Men who will fight for their children, fight for their marriages, fight for the weak and helpless. Men who will never give up, never shut up, and never compromise their walk with God.

Most men have dreamed all their life of being the hero, the one who against all odds defeats an evil ruler, slays a vicious dragon, or saves a beautiful princess. Well… the dream is from God and the hero is you according to Daniel 11:32. "…***but the people that do know their God shall be strong, and do exploits".*** The real key is for us to know our God, so we shall have strength to do exploits! Sounds dangerous, and yet inviting doesn't it? As well it should because that's exactly what it is. It's an invitation from God to the battlefield, a call to arms where we are expected to show up and make a difference. So instead of praying for the answer, we take our rightful place in this battle and become the answer!

We need men who privately walk with God in integrity and righteousness, because what you are privately is what you'll be publicly in time. We need men who are strong in moral character at home. Then we know that they can help us find and maintain our moral compass as a nation. Mature men take responsibility for their actions at home, at work, as well as when no one is looking! I mean real men who are much more interested in having real significance by and through a willingness to help others to become significant, and not just successful.

If there was ever a need for real men to rise up and take back their God-given place in society, this is it. The downward spiral of our country screams for some modern-day knights. Men who will slay the dragon, defeat the evil wizard, and win back the fair maiden. You are that knight! So show up, stand up, build up and never ever give up. Be a real man and in so doing bring glory to God!!!

References:

Chapter 12
1) Courageous Men in Tough Times, By Ed Cole, Published by" Creation House", ISBN# 0-88419-271-7
Pg. 167

What's A Real Man?
ISBN# 978-0-615-94666-5

Other Available Books

Dealing with Death Gods Way:
ISBN# 978-0615351506

Ministry's Not Easy:
ISBN# 9781460986110

Published by Angels/Unaware, LLC